Traditional YORKSHIRE recipes

CATHERINE ROTHWELL

AURORA
PUBLISHING

"To Judith, daughter of a Good Yorkshire Cook"

© This edition AURORA PUBLISHING

ISBN: 1 85926 106 X

DISTRIBUTED BY
Aurora Enterprises Ltd.
Unit 9, Bradley Fold Trading Estate, Radcliffe Moor Road, Bradley Fold, BOLTON BL2 6RT.
Tel: 01204 370753/2   Fax: 01204 370751

WRITTEN BY
© **Catherine Rothwell - 1997**

PRINTED & BOUND BY
MFP Design & Print
Unit E3, Longford Trading Estate, Thomas Street, Stretford, Manchester M32 0JT.
Tel: 0161 864 4540   Fax: 0161 866 9866

FRONT COVER PHOTOGRAPH
Whernside by © Bryan Richards.

Introduction

Collecting Yorkshire recipes is indeed a challenge as Yorkshire must be one of the most famous counties in all Great Britain as far as good cooking is concerned. The other is of course Lancashire! I have a foot in both camps, being Lancashire born and bred and also having relatives in Yorkshire - only just - Todmorden and Bacup in the distant days I speak of being reckoned "Yorkshire". Those of the clan who moved south took the best of Lancashire and Yorkshire cooking with them, wooing southerners away from packets of biscuits. Indeed, in the Surrey of the late 1940s Helen Betts and I waged a campaign, but Helen gave up within two years to return to her native Yorkshire, Surrey, in her opinion, being low on both cooking and hills. Helen's description of bacon and egg pie, eaten tramping over Ingleborough (and I would not put it past her to be) still makes my mouth water.

I have sampled, and cooked meals in Wensleydale, Dentdale, Malhamdale, Ribblesdale and Wharfedale, and though laying no claims to be either chef or gourmet, I cannot think that steak bought in Kirkby Stephen was served up more deliciously anywhere than in our old caravan at Marthwaite, or deep custard pie, rich-gold in colour, tasted better anywhere in the open air than in our secret valley where once Quakers settled wide of Barbon.

The years of history behind some of these recipes are very revealing and to the historian a fascination in themselves. Yorkshire farmhouses are a mine of information: diaries, accounts books, old receipt books, journals send one scurrying home to record and bake. "Ask for Goodall's Yorkshire Relish with your chop or steak" was the mandate in 1895, a year when roast duck and peas, plum pudding, roast pheasant, rabbit pie, fried lapwings' eggs, pigs' feet stew, onion, porridge, spice cake and "good old Yorkshire ham boiled, and home-cured tongue" were on the bills of fare, the last-mentioned from an Otley homestead, where much store was placed on the "set-pot flue".

Yorkshire fare helped on the last railway built by pick and shovel, from Settle to Carlisle. At its centenary celebration in 1976 a menu similar to that at the opening ceremony was served to passengers at Normanton Station: Spring soup; salmon cutlets; steak; jellies and creams and cheese. Round, spiced buns marked with a cross were made by Yorkshire bakers who worked all night ready for early delivery on Good Friday carrying baskets covered with white cloths through the streets. Housewives rose at dawn to do likewise and at Christmas to prepare the Michaelmas goose. "Bought a fat goose in the Cross, weighed 12 pounds and paid tenpence hapenny a pound for it, a lot of money," wrote shrewd Yorkshireman John Dickinson in 1898. On Christmas Day he ate savoury pudding before the goose.

"Cleaning down" or what later was known as Spring cleaning seems to have been the bane of Yorkshiremen's lives 100 years ago, but there was a special slow-cooking stew at the end of the day in a spotless kitchen to compensate. They were men who needed plenty of "bagging", when one considers John Dickinson of Timble. He was registrar of births and deaths, vaccinations, a bacon curer, tea and paraffin seller, waterworks superintendent, insurance agent, hay dealer, manure agent and highways collector.

Closer to my own times I remember with affection another Yorkshireman and cook, Cecil Forrest Doughty, and his description of the autumn family outing before winter set in, travelling on the old Great Eastern Railway through Malton, Pickering, Goathland, and walking to Beck Hole to find the "stands" of filbert nuts. "We filled our knapsacks to bursting point with the ripe nuts which we kept until Christmas, ate raw with salt, roasted or used to decorate cakes - the pilgrimage we made in 1913 was the last as the First World War commenced."

A plate of hot pot at the Fox and Hounds Inn, Guiseley, sounds as delicious as good, warm, potato pie for dinner at Staithes. Yorkshire's landscape, cast in the heroic mould, calls for both with such diversity of contour where hills march away in all directions and valleys are full of sweetness and light. As we walked green roads carved by the pack horse trains or followed the winding rivers the drama and beauty of its scenery unfolded. Needless to say the exertion in all weathers made us ravenous.

Of these recipes old and new collected from all over Yorkshire, the one that "fills me up" most even before I sample it, is the one I shall frame. I have read it over and over again. It weighs in eggs and is headed: "This receipt makes Castle Puddings or small cakes baked in patty tins." I just love that little girl with her instinct of nurture and nourishment whom I always think of as Mary Ann and who, I feel sure, made an excellent wife and mother for some deserving Yorkshire family one whole century ago.

If more proof is needed as to the greatness of this county's cooking, I must quote Charles Dickens who had "a gifted raven from a village public house" sent to him by a friend in Yorkshire. "He had not the least respect for anybody but the cook, to whom he was attached." When taken ill, the bird roosted by the kitchen fire, and the famous novelist reports in his introduction to Barnaby Rudge: "He kept his eye to the last upon the meat as it roasted."

Catherine Rothwell

Traditional Yorkshire Recipes

Contents

Starters & Accompaniments

Main Courses

Contents

Main Courses

Puddings, Desserts & Cakes

Contents

Puddings, Desserts & Cakes

Drinks, etc.

Starters & Accompaniments

FRITTER BATTER

Yorkshire fritters were served for luncheon, dinner or supper, as vegetable or sweet according to ingredients. The basic fritter batter from May Woods is as follows:

½ teaspoon baking powder
1 cup flour
⅔ cup of milk
1 egg

Sift ingredients together. Add beaten egg and milk. Beat until smooth.

As with Yorkshire Pudding, fritters provoked argument. Some favoured a thicker batter similar to that used on coating fish.

Fritters were fried in deep fat, hot enough to brown a piece of bread in one minute. At a lower temperature a soggy fritter resulted, anathema to the Yorkshire cook who in those days had never heard of cholesterol. I remember apple fritters as one of the delights of childhood, but they were a rare treat.

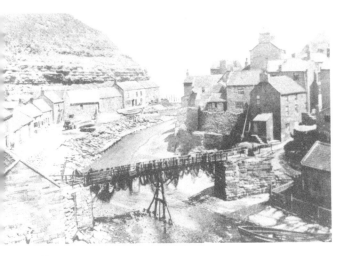

About two miles from Runswick, is the fishing village of Staithes where Captain Cook, the great global navigator, was once employed as grocer's assistant. Grosmont, up the River Esk to Egton and on from Egton Bridge to Glaizedale, led to some picturesque country famous for picnics 100 years ago when this photograph was taken, Beggar's Bridge being the best known place of all. Staithes itself served lobster and freshly caught sea fish to visitors but many of its original cottages have become second homes for the wealthy.

RASPBERRY VINEGAR

Put 1 lb. of fresh raspberries in a china bowl and pour on 1 quart of white vinegar. Next day strain the liquor onto a further pound of fresh raspberries and on the following day do the same but do not squeeze the fruit; only drain the liquor from it and bottle.

To modern eyes this old recipe seems extravagant but many people had bumper crops of raspberries and prized this concentrated drink as a soothing cough medicine, healer of sore throats in the winter time.

Another Yorkshire use for vinegar is on chips. Jimmy Jackson, chief fish frier since 1928 at Harry Ramsden's famous Yorkshire chip shop, reckons that fish have become watery versions of what they used to be.

South Sands at Scarborough is crowded with visitors, bathing vans, tents, vendors' stalls, but Derrick's Black Minstrel Show is attracting most people in this early 1900s postcard. The inevitable "while you wait" photographer will be on the beach somewhere. By means of a small rapid developer tank he could supply an almost instant likeness on thin metal which, although it eventually faded, could capture the moments of sand castles and ice cream very well.

MARY PARKIN'S YORKSHIRE PUDDING

Mix the flour with fresh milk to produce a consistency resembling cream. Beat the 3 eggs well and add quickly to the creamy mixture. At this point there are two schools of thought in Yorkshire. Some say allow the batter to stand for half an hour; others say, "immediately pour it into the pudding tin." All agree that the fat (not much of it) must be very hot. My mother used to pour the meat gravy out of the roasting tin, raise the joint onto a trivet, heat thoroughly a small amount of dripping or lard in the roasting tin and pour the pudding into this 30 minutes before serving the meal. I favour no waiting for the batter. Immediacy seems to make a crisper, lighter pudding, and Mary agrees.

3 tablespoons sieved flour

3 eggs

milk

YORKSHIRE SAUCE

Beat the port with strips of orange peel for about 5 minutes then strain it. Add the other ingredients. Heat for a few minutes, adding the orange juice. Serve it piping hot with hot boiled ham.

1/4 pint port

pinch of cinnamon

1 tablespoon redcurrant jelly

1 tablespoon rich brown gravy

the juice of 1 large sweet orange to be put in last of all

In the background of the cobbled market place of Dent, July 1919, can be seen Adam Sedgwick's memorial; water pouring from under an immense granite slab. Adam was born in Dent in 1785. Francis Edge, who did three peaks in one day, started from Dent in the September of 1947 "with the smell of sizzling bacon floating up from the kitchen" and the "promise of grilled ham" at 6pm in Horton before catching the train home.

YORKSHIRE STUFFING

This stuffing consists of bread soaked in water and squeezed out. Mix in salt, pepper, sage and 2 tablespoons of washed currants. Use this to stuff pork and when the pork is cooked beat into the stuffing an egg yolk and gravy from the roasting tin. This makes a savoury bread sauce to accompany the pork and is recommended by a friend in Leeds.

Before the railways arrived, eight coaches a day ran from Leeds to London. Post wagons carrying goods also left, known as Pickford and Deacon's caravans. In those days the Talbot Inn at Leeds was noted for good food.

DUMPLINGS FOR OLD-FASHIONED BROTH

Mix well with milk to a soft dough. Roll into little balls. Roll in flour and drop in boiling broth just 20 minutes before serving. Eat with broth. "Lovely!"

8 oz. flour

2 teaspoons baking powder

4 oz. suet

4 oz. sultanas

OLD-FASHIONED BROTH

This recipe is for 10 persons so needs to be modified, although a quantity would keep in today's fridges. The large measures are authentic and interesting in themselves. Feeding a family and farm workers round a long, deal table, no doubt it would be finished at one meal.

2 lb. neck or shoulder of mutton

1 teacup barley

1 large Spanish onion, carrot and turnip

1 rabbit

Small amount of dried oatmeal

Put plenty of water in a large broth pot and set on the fire. Meanwhile, clean and joint the rabbit. Drop in barley, mutton and rabbit if young (an old rabbit is better soaked for 12 hours in cold water and salt; the age may be known by its teeth). When broth reboils, drop in the vegetables all cut down and a good bunch of parsley. Take a small handful of oatmeal previously dried in the oven and scatter in with the left hand whilst the broth is boiling briskly and being stirred with a porridge stick. Simmer for 3 hours, adding seasoning at the end. The dumplings are dropped in 20 minutes before serving. Broth was considered the most economical fare to place on the table for a working man and his family.

CHEESE PUDDING

Grate the cheese into the breadcrumbs. Add the other ingredients. After combining well, bake in a moderate oven for half an hour.

3 oz. Wensleydale cheese
5 oz. breadcrumbs
1 pint warm milk
2 well-beaten eggs
a little sea salt

In Queen Elizabeth I's day it was written about the English: "They eat very frequently and are particularly fond of young swans, rabbits, deer and sea birds. They often eat mutton and beef, considered to be better here than anywhere else in the world. They have all kinds of fish in plenty and great quantities of oysters."

A MARINADE FOR BREAM, SALMON OR TROUT

This marinade for bream, salmon or trout is an old recipe used in Yorkshire when salmon was cheap. "That brilliant little river", the Esk, with its seven weirs was particularly good for salmon.

The fish should be dredged with flour and browned in hot oil. Reduce the heat and cook for about 10 minutes. Except for the lemon, the ingredients for the marinade should be gently boiled up together. Simmer on for $^1/_2$ hour then cool. Place the cooked fish in an oblong dish and pour over the marinade with a slice or two of lemon on top. Allow 24 hours, drain and serve.

3 fish whole or in steaks
1 lemon
1 Spanish onion
sprig of fresh rosemary
1 bay leaf
freshly ground sea salt
$^1/_4$ pint white vinegar
$^1/_4$ pint white wine
$^1/_2$ teaspoon ground cinnamon and ground cloves
flour and oil for fish

HARE SOUP

Take an old hare, cleanse, cut the meat into pieces and lay at the bottom of a soup pot with 1¹/₂ lb. lean beef, a slice of lean bacon, an onion, a bunch of sweet herbs. Pour on these, 2 pints of boiling water. Cover the pot and set it into a kettle of water. Simmer "till the hare is stewed to pieces". Strain off the liquor and boil it up quickly with an anchovy, adding sea salt and cayenne to season. Serve in a tureen with small suet dumplings. At Knaresborough in 1880 hares were sold at 6/6d. each and reckoned "a first rate meat dinner".

Knaresborough Castle clings to the banks of the Nidd gorge, a place full of Yorkshire history, home of Blind Jack of Knaresborough, Jack Metcalf, forerunner of the great roadmakers of the 18th. and 19th. centuries. The "Roaring Dillies" could do 90 miles in less than 14 hours but the London to Edinburgh route, passing through Yorkshire, could take up to 18 days if snow occurred. In the midwinter of 1831 the Scottish Mail Coach came off the road in a blizzard, the snow posts having been obliterated. "Blind Jack", a remarkable Yorkshireman, died at Spofforth in 1810, aged 93.

Advertisements for food in such Yorkshire newspapers as "The Dewsbury Reporter", The "Clitheroe Advertiser" and "Times" (which then covered parts of Yorkshire), The "Batley News" and The "Leeds Mercury" in the 1880s offered Scotch whisky at 2s-9d. a bottle, bacon at sevenpence a pound, beer at 1s-6d. a gallon. For joining a Christmas Club at sixpence a week for ten weeks, in the heavy woollen district of Dewsbury members received an iced Christmas cake, raspberry sandwich, $^1/_2$ lb. biscuits, 6 macaroons, a sponge cake, $^1/_2$ lb. mincemeat, 6 mince tarts and $^1/_4$ lb. tea. And that was not all! One of the prettiest pictures that has ever been published, "Life's Springtime", was thrown in also. The reporting staff of the "Dewsbury Reporter" are shown in 1897. The paper, which commenced in 1858, was started by the Woodhead family of Huddersfield.

Main
Courses

A GENUINE YORKSHIRE PORK PIE

Make the pastry as follows:

Melt 2 oz. lard and 2 oz. butter in $1/4$ pint hot water. Boil it. Remove from heat and pour the liquid onto $3/4$ lb. of well sifted flour. Mix it quickly (the kitchen must be warm), beating in an egg. Mince 2 lb. pork with $1/4$ teaspoon rubbed sage.

Line a greased 1 lb. cake tin with the pastry, allowing enough on the side to make the lid later. Fill the pie and cover with pastry lid. Bake for 2 hours in pre-heated moderate oven.

The best stock to add to this traditional pie is made by boiling up 2 pig's trotters with a spoonful of herbs. Pour this through the hole in the pie lid when the pie is cooked and allow the pie to become quite cold before turning it out of the tin.

This pie originated in Huddersfield where the lady cook remembered the days of "Hot Udder Tonight" and similar notices in Sheffield shops. When Daniel Defoe visited Huddersfield in his tour through England he commented on the woollen goods sold there called kersies and that "Oaten bread and oatcakes were the favourite food of the people". In some parts of Yorkshire we heard it spoken of as Riddle Bread.

The good ship "Hornsea" sailed along the Yorkshire coast to the Humber Estuary in the early years of this century. Here are some of her crew on the day of their New Year party, a special one because it heralded the year 1900. As 1899 crept into 1900 all the crew were photographed under a banner bearing the words "A Happy New Year" which they had stretched across the ship. Traditionally, on the stroke of midnight ships sounded their sirens and hooters.

TURBOT WITH FISH SAUCE

Chop up fine the onion and anchovies and put them in the stock with the herbs, crushed peppercorn and thinly cut lemon rind. Boil till reduced to ¹/₂ pint. Melt the butter, add the flour and mix well. Strain on the stock and stir till the sauce boils. Boil for 3 minutes and allow it to cool slightly. Season to taste, add lemon juice and pour onto a well beaten egg. Stir well, strain and serve with boiled turbot, which should be prepared as follows:

l onion
³/₄ pint fish stock
1 bunch fresh herbs
1 oz. butter
1 oz. flour
1 egg
juice and rind of ¹/₂ lemon
2 peppercorns
2 anchovies
1 well beaten egg

Wash the turbot and tie in a piece of muslin. Put into pan containing salt and a tablespoon of vinegar in water sufficient to cover. Bring to the boil and simmer gently for 10 minutes. Cod or fresh haddock can be used instead. Slit the muslin after lifting out the fish with a wide, slatted fish slice. Place fish on a hot dish with a twist of lemon and sprigs of parsley. Serve it with the fish sauce.

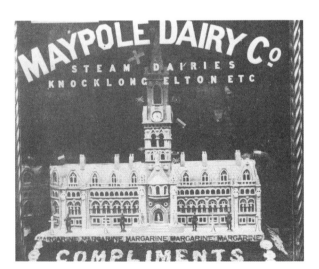

The Corporation of Bradford erected an imposing Town Hall. On the occasion of its opening, the Maypole Dairy Company exhibited in one of their shops in the town, this model carved entirely from margarine. 6 feet long, 2¹/₂ feet high, the tower 6 feet high, weighing over 300 lbs., it took three days to construct. Whether the margarine went into a lot of cakes after the occasion, I could not discover!

GRIDDLED MACKEREL

Fresh mackerel, seasoned, split open and cooked on a griddle over a low, glowing-embered fire (what is called "scrowling" in Cornwall) is one of the unforgettable tastes of my youth. Mackerel poached in salt water is also excellent but the fish has to be mint fresh.

To accompany the griddled mackerel were potatoes done in a special way, resulting in another culinary experience that stayed long in the memory.

Bring about 2 lb. peeled potatoes to the boil and drain. Grease a pie dish with butter and fill it with potatoes. Sprinkle with chopped or rough-cut pieces of 1 small onion. Season, and half fill the dish with some of the water in which the potatoes were boiled. Brush dripping over the potatoes. Cover with greaseproof paper and place in a hot oven, then remove the paper and allow the browning process to take over. The water evaporates, resulting in brown-topped, crisp potatoes with soft, floury bases. Often the Sunday joint of meat was put on top.

This Yorkshire farmer photographed by Joseph Simpson of Sneyd Street, Tunstall in the 1890s also had a number of public duties. He was particularly interested in horses and eventually moved to a farm in Poulton-le-Fylde where many horse sales were held. In the photograph he appears to have his arm on the family bible in which all births and deaths occurring in the family were carefully recorded. Another family standby was Doctor Hill's leather-bound "Family Herbal of 1822". This listed "plants which are remarkable for their virtues ... their description and uses".

Stress was laid on eating plenty of good food in order to keep well. Charles Doughty, a Yorkshire farmer (1809-1899) recommended "good old Yorkshire ham boiled and home-cured tongue". Descended from the Viking Ericsson, he was the last of his line to farm.

Of the Yorkshire farmer it was then jokingly said:

"...would grouse if it rained grass and corn.

To natter and grumble he seems to be born."

MEAT LOAF

"This meat loaf was great for suppers with fried, mashed potato and home-made chutney. At pig-killing times all the bones were scraped clean of meat and then boiled for stock. The meat would be minced, fat as well, and mixed in a big bowl with chopped sage, pepper, salt and breadcrumbs. If we had fresh sage we chopped that in."

3 lb. meat
8 oz. breadcrumbs
1 onion double minced

Mix all this together with 2 beaten eggs to have a soft mixture. Use some pork stock if needed. Have a bread tin ready with very thin belly pork slices. Fill with the mixture, pressing down well. Tie with a floured cloth.

Put tin in a large can holding cold water and bake about 1 hour at 180°C. until firm to touch. Remove from oven and leave to cool with a weight on top. Turn out to serve with salad or the fried, mashed potato and home-made chutney referred to above. "It is delicious enough to make a slimmer throw his diet card through the window."

Esther goes on to say, "my mother used to salt a piece of belly pork for 4 days then roast it and we ate all this cold with jacket potatoes."

RABBIT PIE

In the 1900s some farmers in the Yorkshire Dales could make their rent out of rabbits, the bigger farms catching 3,000 in a season, so the farm workers got plenty of rabbit pies.

The pastry was made with lard - 4 oz. lard rubbed into 9 oz. flour. Line a deep dish with pastry. Put in the rabbit and pork or bacon and dust lightly with pepper and salt. A little stock or water should be added to the dish, the pie covered with a pastry lid and cooked for 2 hours in a moderate oven. Cover the crust with damp greaseproof paper so that it does not over-brown.

Lamb could be substituted for rabbit. An Otley diary from 1881 of a farmer who describes himself as "lish and active" reads: "Home to a very good dinner of lamb pie followed by apple pie."

1 rabbit jointed

3 slices pork or bacon

VENISON WITH SAUCE

Rub the joint of venison well with lard, cover with foil and roast at 180°C, 35 minutes to the pound. Allow to brown towards the end by removing foil.

Sauce

Collect the juices from the roast venison and add the chopped onion, stir in the flour, wine, anchovy and thyme. Cook, stirring all the time until it thickens. Serve with the venison.

1/2 pint red wine

1 onion

1 tablespoon flour

3 teaspoons mashed anchovy

1 teaspoon thyme

Venison was served hundreds of years ago in halls and Mediaeval castles when those "below the salt", i.e. the peasantry, were served "umbles", the entrails of deer. Those above the salt received the roast venison. Personally, I would not care to eat umble pie.

SAUSAGES

Chop 1¹/₂ lb. pork
Chop 1¹/₂ lb. veal with all skin and sinews removed
Add ¹/₂ lb. beef suet (shredded)
Mince and mix together all ingredients
Crumb a penny loaf in water and mix this in, also adding dried sage, pepper and salt.

The age of this Yorkshire recipe is given away by reference to "a penny loaf". 12 oz. breadcrumbs is sufficient for the mixture and about ¹/₂ pint water.

SCARBOROUGH JUGGED HARE

After cleaning and skinning, cut the hare up and season with pepper, salt, spice, pounded mace and nutmeg. Put it into a jar with an onion, a bunch of sweet herbs, a piece of beef and the bones. Tie the jar down with strong parchment paper and place in a saucepan of water up to the neck of the jug. Keep water boiling for 5 hours. Boil the gravy up with a piece of butter and flour prior to serving. Forcemeat balls can be served with jugged hare.

Ripon's 16th. century Wakeman's House has a fine display of local history for the visitor. In the foreground can be seen the Horn Blower near Cafe Lawrence, well known in the late thirties for its Hovis bread. Employed at the Unicorn Inn where he lived until his death was a character known as "Old Boots of Ripon". He would hold a coin between his hooked nose and his turned-up chin to amuse customers. If he held the coin long enough he was allowed to keep it. Thomas Spence was his real name.

NIDDERDALE ROLY POLY

Roll out the suet crust, made from 4 oz. shredded suet and 8 oz. S.R. flour. Add a little water. Sprinkle with seasoning. Place the grated vegetables and sliced tomatoes evenly over the crust. Add more seasoning. Gently roll up the suet pastry containing the vegetables and boil in a pudding cloth for at least 2 hours. Serve with gravy.

3 carrots

1 parsnip

1 turnip

5 small potatoes

some finely chopped celery

3 tomatoes

suet crust and seasoning

TRIPE AND ONIONS

Bring onions to the boil then slice thinly. Wash tripe thoroughly and cut into pieces. Put tripe and onions into a saucepan. Season and cover with the milk and water. Simmer for two hours. Mix the flour to a paste with a little milk and stir into the tripe and onions. Bring to the boil. Simmer on for seven minutes. Serve with plenty of mashed potatoes.

1 lb. tripe

1 pint of milk and water (half and half)

1 oz. flour

2 large onions

salt and pepper

Mrs. Dorothy from Barnsley, who supplied the above recipe, made tripe and onions for her family, and her mother before her, some sixty years ago. Barnsley Market had stall after stall full of all kinds of tripe, cowheel, shin beef and brawn for sale. These formed the basis of many a sound Yorkshire recipe. Barnsley had grown rich from the coal mined there for five hundred years, but now nearly all the pits are closed. The men who for hours on end hewed coal and pushed wagons hundreds of feet below the earth's surface needed a good meal after each shift and this recipe often provided the answer.

The diary of a Dalesman from the village of
Timble records with appreciation
"a good dinner of roast beef, Yorkshire pudding
and new potatoes", June 1889.

YORKSHIRE PUDDING

for TOAD IN THE HOLE

Gradually add well beaten egg and milk to flour, making a well in the centre of the mixing bowl and drawing the flour into the batter. When all the milk has been added use at once. Heat dripping in a roasting tin until very hot, pour off excess and put batter into tin. Cook in a hot oven 250°C. until risen, crisp and golden. Toad in the Hole, the "toads" being sausages, was made by spreading sausages in this Yorkshire Pudding batter.

6 oz. flour
1 pint milk
2 eggs
$^1/_4$ teaspoon salt

STUFFED HEARTS

Obtain 4 sheeps' hearts from the butcher. Wash and stuff them with sage and onion stuffing i.e. old-fashioned forcemeat. Sprinkle with salt and blobs of dripping. Bake them in a hot oven in a covered meat tin for 1$^1/_2$ hours.

How many good Yorkshire cooks are in this photograph from 1901? A section of the Bible Class in their best hats and bonnets are ready to go forth on an outing to Buttercrambe Village woods wide of Selby where fallow and red deer roamed. One lady wearing a muff to keep her hands warm suggests it might be Autumn. On such trips pounds of hazel nuts were gathered, some of which were salted and put aside in jars for Christmas fare.

BAKED STUFFED LIVER

This economical, nourishing dish also used forcemeat, made by chopping sage, onions and breadcrumbs together.

³/₄ lb. sliced lamb's liver
¹/₂ lb. tomatoes
forcemeat stuffing
bacon

Alternate layers of liver, forcemeat and tomatoes are placed in a pie dish with a layer of bacon entirely covering. Greaseproof paper is spread onto this and the dish baked in a moderate oven for 45 minutes.

GRANNY BROWN'S MEAT ROLL

The suet crust for this tasty dish can now be conveniently made by mixing 3 oz. shredded suet with 8 oz. flour and binding with a little water. Granny Brown used to shred a block of suet when she made this in the early 1900s.

Mince 1 lb. stewing beef with 2 onions, seasoning well. Roll out the suet crust. Spread the moistened meat and onion on the crust. Roll up and tie in a floured pudding cloth, allowing room for expansion when the suet swells. Steam for 3 hours. This was a great favourite with the children on the cold days after Christmas. Granny Brown served it with "a brown sauce", the recipe for which has not survived.

POACHED SALMON
WITH LEMON MAYONNAISE

Blend these ingredients together and when well mixed, trickle in at a slow, gradual rate, ³/₄ pint sunflower oil, increasing the rate of flow as the mayonnaise thickens. The juice and zest of 2 lemons completes. The Victorians used olive oil but I think corn oil lighter. Either way this is infinitely better than any bottled commercial preparation. Serve with salmon steaks gently poached in water with a dash of lemon for 12 minutes. Overcooking impairs flavour.

4 egg yolks

2 dessertspoons white vinegar

1 level teaspoon powdered mustard

plenty of freshly milled white peppercorns and sea salt

From Richard Hopper's, Bell Inn, Bland's Cliff, Scarborough, in 1823 a Diligence (coach) ran to Whitby at 8am every Sunday and Wednesday. Horse-drawn coaches and wagonettes were followed by early motor charabancs. The drive is still popular, through Burniston, Cloughton and across the moor. The Children's Corner at Scarborough in 1910 is described by Cissie Hughes on July 19th. as "lovely; there is so much variety. We are staying at the top of a hill overlooking the sea."

VENISON PASTY

Bone a shoulder of venison, beat and season. Mutton fat compensates for the rather dry meat of venison. Bake in a slow oven for 3 hours. Cut the meat in pieces when it has cooled and lay it at the bottom of a pie dish with seasoning and butter. Pack the meat well together. A gravy made by boiling the venison bones can be added to the dish, about $1/2$ pint in quantity. Line the sides of the dish and cover the top with a thick crust of pastry but none should go at the bottom. When the venison pasty comes from the oven pour more hot gravy into it by a funnel in the centre. Shake the dish and serve.

Scott's Pork Butchers in Petergate who also sell York Ham and Bacon; Thomas of York, Baker from old Girdler Gate; Russell's of Coppergate, Purveyors of Fine Food; Betty's of York (we also bought herbs from Culpepper), especially on a late November visit when carols were ringing in the crisp air, certainly conjure up visions of old-fashioned Christmas fare.

In Yorkshire, High Tea, fashionable 100 years ago, was an institution, eaten at 6 o'clock in the evening, unthinkable without York Ham and every possible variety of ginger bread, parkin, teacake and bread. Today's York can still proudly supply them all. My father's tracklements for venison were redcurrant or rowan jelly when the year's home made pickled walnuts were done, but only the last mentioned were tolerated for York Ham.

*J. Biltcliffe and Son of Bridge Street, Penistone,
photographed the local brass band in the 1930s, obviously
on a cup-winning occasion. The Yorkshire brass band was
indispensable for parties, processions, field days and such
occasions as the opening of Whitby and Pickering Railway
on Thursday May 26th. 1836. A crowd assembled outside
the Angel Inn at Whitby. The procession, headed by a brass
band, marched off, followed by the cheery crowd waving
flags. At the station three coach loads of passengers, each
coach drawn by a horse, set off along the gleaming new
rails. This postcard was discovered in Langsett.*

GRANNY IBBETSON'S BRAWN RECIPE

(used also by her mother at Robin Hood's Bay)

Cover with water and cook for 4 hours, simmering slowly, adding onions, bunch of herbs, 4 cloves and 4 peppercorns, 2 bay leaves, the latter 4 ingredients tied up in muslin.

Allow to cool. Remove meat from bones and place in a mould or pudding basin. Strain the stock over the meat and leave on cold pantry shelf to set. Slow simmering is the secret.

¹/₂ lb. shin beef
1 cowheel
¹/₂ lb. ham or oxtail

POTTED BEEF AND HAM
NOVEMBER 1919

"This was my mother's recipe for potted beef and ham. Made on baking day and spread warm on oven bottom cakes with farm butter.

2 lb. shin beef
1 lb. ham

Cover with cold water, add bay leaf and onion. Simmer for 3-4 hours until tender. Skim and strain off the stock. Mince meat three times in mincing machine (no need with a magimix, but must admit the texture is better with the mincing machine). Turn into a bowl, add seasoning and a little of the stock - the rest of the stock made good soup. Press into pots or moulds. When cold, pour melted butter on top to exclude the air."

Folly Dolly Falls, Meltham.

Folly Dolly Falls, Meltham near Huddersfield, July 1907. What better place for grand scenery and a picnic? Other magnificent waterfalls in Yorkshire are Kisdon Force and Hardrow Force the latter a mile from Hawes, where the finest fall in the county leaps sheer from a height of 80 ft. Here, as at Ingleton, it is possible to walk behind the waterfall as so much rock has been worn away, but in severe weather it has been known to become one huge icicle.

Hardraw was notable for its acoustic properties and in the days when every village had a brass band, contests were held here. The Green Dragon Inn was kept busy feeding the multitudes.

VEGETABLE PASTY FROM GOATHLAND

Left over potatoes and turnips were mashed well together with a knob of butter seasoned with salt and pepper and chopped parsley added. Rounds of pastry were filled down one side, another small pat of butter placed in each, the edges wetted and the pasty closed securely by crimping together the wetted edges. The tops of the pasties were brushed with beaten egg to produce a tempting golden look.
I think these old-fashioned vegetable pasties are even better with a little cooked, chopped onion added to the filling.

The pastry was made as follows:

Rub fat into flour until the mixture resembles breadcrumbs. Add the water and mix into pastry, adding a little water at a time. The pastry should come cleanly away from the bowl. Iced water was used but we get good results today by placing in the fridge for an hour at the "breadcrumb" stage.

1 lb. strong white flour
8 oz. lard
¼ pint water

BEEF AND POTATO PIE

Cut up beef and place in a pan with ½ pint water, the chopped onion and seasoning. Bring to boil and simmer for 1 hour. Put in the peeled, cut up potatoes and swede, cooking on until vegetables are done. Keep moist by adding more water. Put all from the pan into a deep pie dish. Make a thick, pastry pie lid and cook at 200°C. for about ½ hour until pie lid is golden brown.

1 lb. stewing beef or skirt
1½ lb. potatoes
1 large onion
½ small swede
1½ lb. shortcrust pastry
pepper and salt
¾ pint water

Eighteenth century Harewood House, home of the Earl of Harewood, was designed by Robert Adam although the original building and estate village were the work of York architect John Carr. The staff of such a large house in the 1880s had to work very hard. The annual wage for a housemaid was £18-£25; for a nursemaid £8-£14; kitchen maid £10-£18; butler £20-£40 and cook-housekeeper £20-£50, An enormous number of staff were employed as page boys; footmen; head chef; second chef; hall porter; kitchen porters; laundry maids; gardeners etc., but perhaps the vegetable and scullery maid had the worst job. Six or seven courses were sent up for dinner parties and she had to work spinach, sauces and chicken through a sieve, peel vegetables and wash greasy pots and pans besides boiling up pudding cloths.

PUFF PASTE SAUSAGE ROLLS

Yes, it used to be called puff paste a hundred years ago and was made as follows:

To every pound of flour, allow the yolk of 1 egg, juice of 1 lemon, 1 lb. unsalted butter, and iced water. Lay the flour on the paste board, make a well in the centre into which you put the yolk of egg and the lemon juice. Mix all this with iced water, adding the latter a little at a time. You do not want a sticky paste. Use the flat of the hand but with as little handling as possible. Roll out the paste and put the butter on it, folding the edges together with the butter inside. Roll out, fold over $^1/_3$, roll lightly, fold another $^1/_3$, roll lightly. Shake a little flour under and over and repeat the folding and rolling process. Flour a baking sheet and leave the rolled-out pastry on this for $^1/_2$ hour in as cold a place as possible. Roll out and turn it, then put back in cool place. Do this about 6 times, reducing the resting time to $^1/_4$ hour, then the paste should be ready.

To make the sausage rolls you need:

I lb. sausage meat

yolk of 1 egg

The puff paste can be rolled out and divided into 12 squares. Place sausage meat on one half of square, wet edges of paste and fold together. Brush each with yolk of egg and bake in hot oven at 200°C. for about $^1/_2$ hour.

Grandmother was said to "get into a swither" over this paste-making together with her other chores, and I'm not surprised!

Traditional Yorkshire Recipes

MUKER. SWALEDALE.

24382

*Brentwood Lodge at Muker in Swaledale offered board residence
with good Yorkshire fare in the 1940s. A Morris Minor motor car
is parked outside the hotel in this quiet village with its old
church and stone buildings whilst on the right the village
carpenter saws through a plank of wood. A signpost points to
Hawes via Buttertubs Pass and to Kirkby Stephen set in lovely
moorland scenery characteristic of Swaledale.*

STEWED OX CHEEK FROM BRADFORD

"Soak and cleanse a fine cheek the day before it is to be eaten; put it into a stew pot that will cover close with 3 quarts of water. Simmer steadily after first boiling and skim. In two hours put plenty of carrots, leeks, turnips and sweet herbs into the stew pot. Four ounces of allspice and one teaspoon of pepper should also be added. Skim often. When the meat is tender take it out and cover it securely.

When the soup goes cold, remove the cake of fat and serve it with the cold meat, browning the gravy with burnt sugar if a darker brown is wanted. Celery is a great addition and should always be served with ox cheek."

This is another "receipt" from early in the 19th. century.

Inspired by a refreshing cup of Taylor's of Harrogate tea, we discovered this interesting photograph of Farrah's Original Harrogate Toffee Shop in the year 1840. The elegant spa town of Harrogate, only three miles from Knaresborough, has beautiful open spaces, gardens and shops, a great contrast in style when fresh from visiting How Stean Gorge or Brimham Rocks, 1,000 feet up, the best example of wind erosion in Britain: millstone grit sculptured into fantastic shapes; Idol Rock, the largest, weighing 200 tons, but resting on a base only 12 inches wide.

FARRAH'S ORIGINAL HARROGATE TOFFEE SHOP IN THE YEAR 1840.

STEWED TRIPE FROM SHEFFIELD

Stew in milk until tender with finely chopped onions or fry the tripe in small pieces dipped in batter. Serve either way in a hot tureen with butter sauce. Soused tripe was made by boiling until not quite tender and putting in salt and water that had to be changed every day until all used. Portions of the soused tripe were dipped in flour and eggs batter and fried until golden brown. Those many years ago people were familiar with several kinds of this succulent food: elder, wezzel, seam, rag and honeycomb, all with distinctive flavours and appearances.

FRIED COW HEEL FROM HUDDERSFIELD

Cow heel and calves' feet could be had very cheaply but the rich jelly they produced told the thrifty housewife that they contained nutriment for her family. One 19th. century recipe treats as follows:

"Soak them well, boil and serve in a napkin with this sauce."
Thick melted butter
A large spoonful of vinegar
A small ladle of mustard and the same of salt.

Pound well together and place in a sauce boat to accompany the cow heel.

Cow heels could also be stewed in brown gravy or vegetable stock, or the heel cut into 4 parts, dipped in egg and fried in butter. Fried onions were the favourite accompaniment.

TED ELLIS'S ROOK PIE

Rook shooting was common in the 1840s and when rookeries were cleared in Spring the birds were collected in sackfuls and made into pies, only the breasts being used as the rest is inedible.

Soak the rooks' breasts for 4-5 hours in lightly salted cold water or diluted milk. The pie dish should be greased and the breasts laid on a bed of good beefsteak, a scattering of salt, pepper and nutmeg, strips of bacon fat and a light dredging of flour. Half fill the dish with water and cover with foil. Bake in a moderate oven for 1¹/₂ hours. The dish should be allowed to cool then be covered with a pastry lid and further cooked in a hot oven for 25 minutes. The steak makes a splendid rich gravy within the pie.

The village of Bolton Abbey is much older than the famous ruin, which is not really an Abbey but a Priory, pictured here in the 1930s. The extensive ruins include cloister, chapter house, prior's lodging and church. What were the Priory's fishponds remain as hollows. The rectory, built about 1700, includes part of the infirmary. For a time Mary, Queen of Scots, was a prisoner at Bolton Abbey.

HOG'S PUDDING

Boil a quart measure of groats in as much milk as will swell them. Add 1 pint of rich cream, 1 lb. of finely chopped parboiled liver and 1/2 lb. of finely minced suet. Use a mixture of herbs thus: grated nutmeg, 6 cloves, spoonful of pepper, spoonful of allspice, handful of parsley, 10 leaves of sage, sprig of thyme, 2 leeks, 1 spoonful of marjoram, 1/2 teaspoon of crushed garlic - all mixed fine. Mix well also 1/2 lb. of breadcrumbs scalded in milk, 8 well-beaten eggs and 2 lbs. of hog's fat. Mix all well together, adding more milk to make the right consistency if needed. This pudding to be boiled or filled in skins as in Black Puddings.

Served at "Aunt Mary's pig feast" last century, varied by a supper of "spare rib and pork leaves" (layers of fat bacon). The men drank "cleat wine with cheese".

On winter visits we spent many an hour talking in the kitchen of Beckside Farm, sides of home-cured bacon hanging above our heads, a roaring fire inside and the wind howling outside, hens and goats snuggled down for the night. In summer it was the coolness of the big kitchen that beckoned, along with Mary's scones. I vividly recall in the heatwave summer of 1976 emerging from White Scar Caves to a vista of white limestone shimmering in heat.

MARTHWAITE BLACK PUDDINGS

The blood of the pig is collected and stirred with a handful of salt till cold. Take a quart of the blood and a quart measure of groats to soak together overnight. Soak the crumbs of a small loaf in 2 quarts of hot milk. The guts of the animal must be well washed, turned in salt and scraped, the water changed several times. Chop a collection of herbs: pennyroyal, pepper, salt, spice, ginger, nutmeg, cloves, and mix with 3 lbs. of shredded beef suet and 6 well-beaten, strained eggs. Beat all these with the bread, groats etc. and as you fill the skins, place pieces of hog's fat at intervals. Tie in links and boil in a large kettle, pricking them or they will burst. Lay between clean cloths until cold. If there are no skins the black pudding mixture can be boiled in pudding basins covered with floured cloths. Slice and fry when ready for use.

KEBOBBED MUTTON

The Victorian cook talked of "kebobbing" meat and dealt with mutton this way:

Remove all the fat and skin. Joint it at every bone. Mix grated nutmeg with salt, pepper, herbs. Dip the steaks of mutton into the yolks of 3 eggs and dust with the seasoning mixture. Place the steaks together on a small spit. Roast by a quick fire, basting well with butter and dusting with more of the seasoning. Lay the "kebobbs" in a dish containing 1/2 pint of gravy made from the meat juices and butter to which has been added 2 teaspoons of ketchup, keeping the meat hot till the gravy is ready.

EY, THE SANDS.

Nowhere along the Yorkshire coast did the ancient way of life persist so tenaciously as at Filey. The old fishing families were the Camishes, Jenkinsons and Boyntons whose nicknames were carried on within the family from generation to generation. Charlotte Brontë loved the atmosphere of Filey and often stayed at Cliff House in Belle Vue Street, then the most southern house in the town.

This 1900s scene shows the sands, firm and golden, five miles of them sweeping a bay backed by precipitous cliffs. Lobsters, shrimps, crabs and fresh fish would be enjoyed by this crowd.

JELLIED PIG'S FEET

Boil the feet in milk after cleaning well. Then boil again in a small quantity of water till every bone can be taken out. Throw in a handful of chopped sage and a handful of parsley, pepper and salt and simmer till the herbs are well scalded.

An 1830 receipt for BUBBLE and SQUEAK
"Boil, chop and fry with a little butter, pepper and salt, some
cabbage, and lay it in slices of beef lightly fried."

STEWED SWEETBREADS

Blanch, and stuff with a forcemeat of chicken fat, lean bacon, anchovy and parsley. When well mixed, add the yolks of 2 eggs. Fill the sweetbreads with the stuffing, fastening them together with skewers, and lay in a pan with slices of veal over and bacon under them. Season with pepper, salt, herbs and a blade of mace. Cover with 2 pints of broth and stew gently for 2 hours. Take out the sweetbreads, strain and skim the broth and boil it down to half a pint. Warm the sweetbreads in it and serve with a slice of lemon.

STUFFED SHOULDER OF LAMB

Have the shoulder ready boned and make the stuffing thus:

2 oz. chopped ham

3 oz. shredded suet

1 teaspoon chopped mint

Mix this with 8 oz. breadcrumbs, bringing about a stuffing consistency by adding milk. Roll the shoulder containing the stuffing and sew up tightly. Put in a casserole with 2 sliced onions and 1 pint stock which should contain the bones removed from the shoulder. Cook for 2 hours in a moderate oven and just before serving take the liquor from the casserole and boil it up quickly to pour over the lamb, served with peas fresh from the pod.

1 teaspoon chopped parsley

LIVER HOT POT WITH PICKLED BEETROOT

Place liver, onions and potatoes in layers in a casserole, sprinkling each layer with seasoning and herbs, ending with a layer of potatoes. Mix the flour and water together and add to the casserole. Bake for almost 2 hours in a moderate oven, in the last half hour placing rashers of bacon on top of the liver hot pot. The beetroots should be prepared in advance, boiled and skinned, taking care not to bruise or pierce them. Allow to cool, slice and pour over them sufficient malt vinegar to cover.

1 large chopped onion

1¹/₂ lb. sliced potatoes

1 dessertspoon flour

¹/₂ pint water

³/₄ lb. sliced liver

seasoning, sage, thyme

MAY·THIS·BIRTHDAY· ·TAKE·THE·CAKE·

D.McG.

IN SENDING YOU THIS BIRTHDAY CAKE I WISH YOU WEALTH & HEALTH BUT I SHANT BE THERE TO SHARE IT SO I TOOK A SLICE MYSELF.

"May this birthday take the cake."

A birthday card sent by a Yorkshire boy's mother in September 1917 "in remembrance of the coming day". No doubt her son was away in Flanders during World War I. Queen Victoria was known to send bars of chocolate in tin boxes to her troops during the Boer War but a slice of Yorkshire birthday cake would have been even more mouth-watering.

Puddings, Desserts & Cakes

ALICE NIGHTINGALE'S FRITTERS

Mix 2 well beaten, strained eggs with milk and flour, sufficient to make one thick pancake. Fry the pancake then pound it in a mortar, adding the yolks of 4 and the whites of 2 eggs, one spoonful of orange flour water, 2 oz. of sugar and grated nutmeg. Pound it all until smooth.

Place 4 oz. lard in a frying pan and heat until smoking. Drop in portions of batter and as they brown, turn them over. Place them in a warm oven or by the fire on sheets of parchment paper. Serve like pancakes as quickly as possible with fruit jelly, stewed fruit or sugar and lemon.

MADEIRA BUNS

Mix all, first working the butter into the sugar. Beat for half an hour, then add one wine glass of sherry. Bake in buttered patty tins in a moderately quick oven.

In 1825, Bradford, from where this recipe came, had a record turn out for the Procession of Bishop Blaize, patron saint of wool combers who in the 19th. century earned 20 shillings a week and worked 12 hours a day.

8 oz. butter

2 well beaten eggs

12 oz. flour

6 oz. sugar

1 large spoonful caraway seeds

1 teaspoon ginger

1 wine glass of sherry

"A BEAUTIFUL PRESERVE OF APRICOTS" Receipt from 1832"
"Choose the finest, ripe apricots, pare them as thinly as
possible and weigh. Lay them in halves on dishes with the
hollow part upwards. Have ready an equal weight of loaf
sugar finely pounded. Strain the sugar over the apricots.
Break the stones from the fruit and blanch the kernels. After
12 hours place all in a preserving pan. Allow it to simmer
until clear jewel-like. Take out the apricots singly and place in
small pots, pouring the syrup and kernels over them. Cover
with waxed discs moistened in brandy."

"Wakefield is a very lively market town, well served of fish
and flesh ... a right honest man shall fare well for two pence
a meal," wrote the chronicler Leland.

Another view of Dent, from the south, photographed in the 1940s by Lilywhite Ltd. of Brighouse, reminds one that in the 17th. and 18th. centuries Dent was a busy knitwear centre. Even shepherds knitted stockings, jerseys and coats, which were taken to Kendal by cart or pack mule. Abraham Dent of Kirkby Stephen, shopkeeper, was also a dealer in knitted stockings and a wine and spirit merchant. As a shopkeeper he sold tea, sugar, flour, books and patent medicines. Abraham also bought wool to be knitted up in Dent and Kirkby Stephen. The stockings made from this he sold mainly to the army. Thomas Pearson delivered "75 dozen hose by first waggon" and must have brought a gift by return, for Abraham Dent writes, "I thank you for the cockles you sent me."

45

OATCAKES

Warm 2 pints of water to blood heat. It must not be too hot. Add the crumbled yeast and a little sea salt then the dry ingredients, stirring in and beating well until the mixture looks like Yorkshire pudding batter, then allow it to stand in a warm place so that the yeast can work. If the mixture seems too thick add a little warmed milk. Grease a griddle, heat well and pour half a cup of the mixture into the centre. Cook for 7 minutes, turn over and cook the other side for 5 minutes. Place the oatcakes on a wire sieve to cool. Some people fry the oatcakes after a day or two, but my father had only one way with oatcakes. He hung them on the rack above the kitchen fire, dried them until crisp, then broke off portions to butter thickly and spread with golden syrup.

1 lb. oatmeal
8 oz. wholemeal flour
¹/₂ oz. baking powder
1 oz. fresh yeast

A sign on Halifax station, "Horses at Work - National Museum of the Working Horse", brought to mind my old departed Quaker friend, Richard Clegg, born 118 years ago in Halifax. He worked with horses all his life, respected their intelligence ("horse sense") and believed that plenty of oats in the diet of both men and horses was good.

LARDY CAKE

Make a dough from the following ingredients:

Allow the dough to rise as bread. Turn onto a floured board and use the filling as follows:

Dab 2 oz. lard over the top $^2/_3$ of the dough. Sprinkle on 1 oz. sugar and 1 oz. currants.

Fold up lower $^1/_3$ of dough, tap $^1/_3$ down, seal edges. Quarter turn the dough, re-roll and repeat with another 2 oz. lard, 1 oz. currants and 1 oz. sugar. The method is just like making flaky pastry. Roll lardy cake to fit a square 8 inch tin. Place in tin and prove. Brush the top with milk and water; scatter with sugar. Bake half way down hot oven for 30 minutes at 220°C. Test by tapping base and listen for hollow sound. Cool on a wire tray. This is best served with butter and was a favourite in the "butty box" for workmen. "Clap" cake and short cake were old Dales terms, the first a cake made from lard and oatmeal, the second, pastry.

$^1/_2$ lb. plain flour
1 level teaspoon salt
$^1/_2$ oz. yeast
$^1/_2$ oz. lard
1 teaspoon sugar
$^1/_4$ pint warm water

ILKLEY TEA CAKE

The fruit must be soaked for one day in strong, milkless tea; the dry ingredients well sifted.

Cream butter and sugar until light and fluffy. Beat in the egg. Fold into the mixture the sifted flour, spice and soda. Lastly stir in the drained, soaked, dried fruit and bake in a floured cake tin for one hour at 180°C.

Ilkley, in ancient Skyrack Wapentake, was noted for "the delicious coldness of its springs and the pure bracing air".

8 oz. sultanas
8 oz. self raising. flour
4 oz. butter
4 oz. sugar
1 teaspoon bicarbonate of soda
1 egg
1 cup of tea without milk
1 teaspoon spice

RYEDALE APPLE PUDDING

Cook the apples slowly, after peeling and coring. When they are fallen and very soft, beat in the sugar and butter and add the lemon peel. Whip the egg whites until stiff and fold into the cooked puree. Pour into a pie dish greased with butter and cover with a lid of puff paste. Bake in hot oven, 200° C. for 20 minutes. A century later this was called apple tart, but other versions e.g. orange or lemon pudding are what we now call pie or cake. "What's for pudding?" must be a very old question from the days when all "sweets" were referred to as puddings.

6 cooking apples
4 egg whites
4 oz. butter
8 oz. puff paste
4 oz. sugar
grated lemon peel

SPICY GINGERBREAD

Mix flour and ginger together. Melt treacle and add sugar, butter and milk. Stir well. Pour into the flour mixture, stirring all the time, or let a mixer do the job. A well-greased, lined cake tin is the best container. Bake in a slow oven 160°C. for just under 1 hour. Turn out and cool when the gingerbread has been out of the oven for 15 minutes.

1 lb. flour
6 oz. butter
1 teaspoon ground ginger
4 oz. sugar
8 tablespoons black treacle
3 tablespoons milk
1 teaspoon baking powder

The old recipe had no baking powder mentioned, but I thought it better to add some. Also, we preferred half golden syrup and half black treacle, but this is a matter of taste. Gingerbread varies greatly according to oven temperature, but if you have to put it in a hotter oven for economy reasons when other dishes are being cooked, it will not spoil provided you do not allow it to burn. It will however have a different texture.

MARY ANN'S CASTLE PUDDINGS

Whip the 4 eggs for 5 minutes then add the sugar, then add the two flours (referring to the ground rice as flour) which must be well mixed together. Add a little salt. Whip the butter to a cream. Add this just before it is put into the oven.

This receipt makes either Castle Puddings or small cakes baked in patty tins."

I used an oven setting of 180° C.

The weight of 2 eggs in:
- *ground rice*
- *2 eggs in flour*

The weight of 4 eggs:
- *in loaf sugar*

The weight of 3 eggs:
- *in butter*

the grated peel of 1 lemon

AINS ABBEY FROM THE EAST

We visited Fountains Abbey and Studley with friends from Bewerley on one of the loveliest days in the summer of 1987. This real photograph from the 1930s shows the dramatic setting chosen by the monks. The Cistercian monks of Jervaulx Abbey made the first Wensleydale cheese from ewes' milk and they also bred horses. Yorkshire, quoted centuries ago as "one tenth of all England", was said to be "a great county for horses".

Fields in the Leeds, Batley and Morley area once supplied half of the country's rhubarb. To "force" it, Yorkshire "tusky" was also grown under buckets on allotments, fertilised with soot of which there was plenty in those days. This rhubarb pudding recipe came from a Yorkshire mill town about 80 years ago but I substitute butter and choose what my grandmother used to call "apple rhubarb", for best flavour.

RHUBARB PUDDING

Produce a shortcrust pastry by rubbing the butter into the flour. Roll out into a 10 inch square and spread the jam (I used home-made plum). Mix the cleaned, chopped rhubarb (do not skin) with the 4 oz. sugar. Roll it all up and place in a greased, oblong casserole. Over the roly-poly shape pour the milk and sprinkle the tablespoon of brown sugar. Bake at 170° C for 50 minutes and you have a light, delicious pudding in its own sauce.

1 lb. apple rhubarb
½ pint milk
4 oz. sugar
4 tablespoons jam
8 oz. plain flour
1 tablespoon brown sugar
4 oz. butter

Mrs. Kay, Grandma Campey's mother, photographed in William Smith's, a studio at Park Lane, Leeds, wears typical matron's dress, Victorian metal beadwork, velvet, fringes and ribbon. Grandfather Campey's portrait from Hunslet Road was too faded to print, both being over 100 years old. Mrs. Kay and Mrs. Campey would know the newspaper "Leeds Mercury", the Royal Exchange built in their time between 1826 and 1829, and recall the laying on August 17th. 1853 of the foundation stone of Leeds Town Hall with its Italian-style architecture. Mrs. Kay's meat pies were served at the Talbot Inn, Leeds.

CURD TART

Whitsuntide is the time for Yorkshire curd tarts. To make the curds, heat a pint of milk almost to boiling point then put in a teaspoon of fresh lemon juice. Stir until the milk curdles and leave overnight in a warm place, covered with a cloth. Strain off the whey next day.

Mix the curds with the currants and lemon. Beat eggs well and stir in with sugar and melted butter. Line a dish with pastry and put the curd mixture in, topping with a flurry of cinnamon or nutmeg (just a whisper). Bake in a moderate oven till set, which usually takes 25 minutes. The year we collected recipes Christopher Woodcock, Master Baker, was one of the six finalists in the county for the best bakery. His family at York have been bakers for 250 years.

8 oz. curds

4 oz. sugar

3 oz. currants

2 eggs

grated lemon rind

knob of butter

shortcrust pastry

A fine photograph of Micklegate Bar, York, with clear indications of the early days of this century: Warriner's Cycle Works and Garage, Pullars of Perth, Shaving. In 1854 a stone tablet inscribed "Erected by the 9th. Legion by Order of Emperor Trajan" was found in York. Eleventh century York was besieged by Normans and Danes and the 20th. century has uncovered a 10th. century Viking Village, now called the Jorvik Centre, in Coppergate, attracting thousands of visitors, as does the National Railway Museum where 150 years of British Railway History can be explored.

Newborough Bar with the Harkness Watch and Clock Company on the right (they were also jewellers) and the Bull Hotel on the left, 1880, is another fine view from this ancient capital of the Roman province of Britain. York, or Eboracum, is one of the oldest cities mentioned by geographer Ptolemy in A.D. 161. It was the capital of the Brigantes tribe until conquered by Agricola. The outline of a Roman camp was discovered on the moors near Leeds in 1702. Wades Causeway at Pickering, urns and inscriptions at Malton and in the valley of the Nidd and along a strongly marked line of Roman roads prove that Yorkshire was one of the busiest stamping grounds of the Romans.

Not far from York Minster we found Jim Garraby's Fudge Kitchen where Toffee, Rum and Raisin, Chocolate, Orange, Ginger and Walnut Fudge was made fresh daily. "See it made" read the notice and we did, sampling the delicious confection. The cook told us she herself liked casseroled food in wine, not having a sweet tooth. Although we did not manage a fudge recipe, this old-fashioned Yorkshire Toffee Apples recipe is a good second best for the Autumn, a time when apples were sold at fairs in York, Knaresborough, Bingley, Wakefield and Bradford.

TOFFEE APPLES

Melt the butter. Add the treacle and sugar and stir gently till it boils. In 15 minutes, when a spoonful is dropped in water it hardens. Allow it to cool a little. Wash and wipe apples, remove any stalks and stick a wooden skewer in each. Dip in the thickened toffee and place upright in a jar on a plate, allowing toffee apple to set.

1 lb. small eating apples
1 lb. treacle
4 oz. butter
1 lb. demerara sugar
6-8 sharpened wooden skewers - these were obtainable from the butcher

TRADITIONAL SPICE CAKE

Grease an 8 inch diameter cake tin. Set oven at 180° C. Sift the first four ingredients. Cream butter and sugar together until fluffy. Beat in syrup and eggs with a little flour. Fold in remaining flour and buttermilk to ensure a smooth consistency. Turn into cake tin and bake in centre of oven for 1 hour 10 minutes. Turn out and cool on a rack. Dust with icing sugar.

9 oz. S.R. flour
¹/₄ level teaspoon cloves
¹/₄ teaspoon cinnamon
pinch of black pepper
4 oz. butter
4 oz. dark soft brown sugar
3 oz. golden syrup
¹/₄ pint buttermilk
2 eggs

A Yorkshire woman, born in Poppleton and a typical good Yorkshire cook, is Joan Ibbetson, who especially loves Appletreewick and Burton Agnes from where come the last two recipes. "Yorkshire Scones" was collected 30 years ago when my sister and I stayed at the Jerry and Ben Cottage near Grassington.

YORKSHIRE SCONES

Sift together the flour, baking powder, sugar and salt. Rub in the butter lightly. Add the milk to the whisked eggs and pour onto dry ingredients gradually. On a floured board roll out the dough to ¹/₂ inch thickness and cut into pieces 3 inches square. Fold over to make a three-cornered scone, brush with milk, dust with sugar and bake for 25 minutes in a hot oven. A really hot oven forms a pleasant crusty outside but maintains soft texture inside. Raisins, currants or sultanas can be added for a change.

2 cups wholemeal flour
3 teaspoons baking powder
1 teaspoon salt
2 tablespoons butter
2 tablespoons sugar
2 eggs
¹/₃ cup milk

YORKSHIRE FAT RASCALS

Sieve flour with the baking powder. Rub in butter and lard. Stir in currants. With the liquid, mix to a stiffish paste and roll out ¹/₂ inch thick. Cut into rounds and bake in a hot oven, 200°C. for 20 minutes. Sprinkle with the sugar and spice.

More argument! The Lancashire side claim this as their own but Yorkshire is adamant that Fat Rascals originated in Yorkshire and I can well believe it, recalling that the county was once country-famed for gargantuan pies. These were made to celebrate special events like the Battle of Waterloo and the Repeal of the Corn Laws, Queen Victoria's Jubilee and the raising of £1,000 for Huddersfield Infirmary. "Raising a pie" successfully was the test of a superlative cook. The Denby Dale 6¹/₂ ton pie contained 5 bullocks and one ton of potatoes.

1 teaspoon baking powder
1 lb. flour
¹/₄ lb. butter
¹/₄ lb. lard
1 teaspoon allspice
1 teaspoon caster sugar
handful of washed currants
a little sour milk and water

urch Street, Ilkley.

Church Street, Ilkley in the early years of this century when milk, warm and fresh from the cow, was brought round in metal churns. People came from their houses armed with jugs and whatever they required was measured out. The milk float in this scene has stopped opposite the Creamery. Deliveries of fresh milk were made morning and evening, the churns and measures being scalded regularly to ensure cleanliness, otherwise the milk would have turned sour.

Ilkley, once a Roman station, was favoured by invalids for its magnificent moorland air. They stayed at such places as Craiglands Hydro. Hydropathy was introduced in 1843 by a Mr. Stansfield and Ilkley became known as "the town of Hydros".

55

GRIDDLE CAKES

Mix and sift the dry ingredients. Add milk and melted butter. Beat well. Bake on a slightly greased hot griddle. A thick, iron frying pan can be used. Turn the cakes once only and use only enough fat to prevent sticking.

2 cups flour

1½ cups milk

4 teaspoons baking powder

2 tablespoons butter

The stone steps in Arguments Yard, Whitby, photographed in the 1920s, looks similar to those leading to the Varley brothers' workshop which I recall in the 1940s in the same town. Up worn steps which passed the cottage where Mary Linskill, Whitby novelist, was born; generations before craftsmen worked in the same premises, carving jet. Of an old Whitby family, great-grandfather Varley was a schoolmaster at Sneaton. The brothers used walnut, mahogany, boxwood, tulipwood, and rosewood to produce works of art in their cabinet-making. The Varleys' cottage had window frames made of teak from the wreck Rohilla.

RIPON APPLE CAKE

Apple Pie and Cheese is typical Yorkshire fare but this treats the ingredients differently.

Line a tin with pastry made as follows:

Rub lard into flour until it resembles breadcrumbs. Bind with a little water. Peel and slice some cooking apples and place on the pastry about 1 inch deep then cover with syrup, sprinkle with a little grated cheese and cover the pie with a pastry lid. Bake in a hot oven at 200° C. for about 35 minutes.

8 oz. lard
1 lb. flour
¹/₄ teaspoon salt

The Bronte Waterfall at Haworth, photographed in September 1905, was a favourite place for visitors to walk to and sit beside for a picnic. It is highly reminiscent of a waterfall we visited above Cray in Upper Wharfedale. Today's visitors to Haworth enjoy Ponden Mill in the heart of Bronte land, the most famous textile mill in the north of England, where linen bargains are hunted. Similar shops are to be found in Harrogate, Leeds, Huddersfield, York, Wakefield.

DORIS BARKER'S MINCEMEAT

"A very juicy, traditional family recipe dating from 1880.

Mix all ingredients together. I add 1 tablespoon brandy."

12 oz. currants

10 oz. sultanas

10 oz. raisins

1 lb. cooking apples minced

rind and juice of 2 large lemons

1 teaspoon mixed spice

HARVO BREAD
(AN OLD YORKSHIRE RECIPE)

Put these in pan and bring to boil. Simmer for 15-20 minutes.

Whilst cooling, put into a bowl :

1 lb. sultanas

¹/₂ lb. butter

1¹/₂ cups sugar

2 cups cold water

Mix together, make hole in centre, then pour lukewarm pan contents in.
Mix well but don't beat.
2 loaf tins, 1¹/₂ hours altogether.
This was baked in a fire oven, but for today - 15 minutes at 180°C., then 140-150°C. for rest of time.

4 cups plain flour

6 teaspoons baking powder

2 teaspoons bicarb soda

1 teaspoon ground ginger

A "jaggin" in Yorkshire Dales dialect is a small load carried in panniers, packs or little carts used by the hill farmers, which travelled between market towns and villages. Old Doncaster Market is shown almost a century ago. In South Yorkshire the town became best known for its railway works, heavy industry and butterscotch toffee. It is an ancient settlement tracing its history back to Roman times. Saxon weapons, 300 million year-old fossils and Roman ornaments are displayed in Doncaster Museum. Its Mediaeval church was gutted by fire in 1853.

VANILLA CREAM SANDWICH

Beat butter and sugar well. Add the beaten eggs gradually and fold in sieved flour and flavouring. Divide mixture between two well greased sandwich tins. Bake for 20 minutes at 180°C. When cold, sandwich together with cream and dredge sparkling fine sugar on top.

4 oz. butter
4 oz. caster sugar
2 eggs
4 oz. S.R. flour
¹/₂ teaspoon vanilla essence

MYSTERY CAKE

Cream butter with sugar and then add beaten eggs. Mix and beat well. Add half of the flour, baking powder, salt and spices, then the milk and all the rest.

In 2 greased layer tins, i.e. sandwich tins, place two thirds of the mixture. In a third tin place the rest of the mixture, to which has been added 1 tablespoon cocoa mixed with 1 tablespoon boiling water. Bake all three "layers" in a hot oven for 15-20 minutes.

¹/₂ cup butter
1 cup sugar
2 eggs
¹/₄ teaspoon salt
4 teaspoons baking powder
1 teaspoon nutmeg
1 teaspoon cinnamon
1 cup milk
2 cups flour

The following is placed between the layers and on top of the cake:

Cream butter then add sugar and cocoa slowly, beating until fluffy. The vanilla and coffee should be added a few drops at a time, making the filling soft enough to spread easily between layers.

2 tablespoons butter
2 cups fine-ground sugar
1 tablespoon cocoa
1 teaspoon vanilla extract
3 tablespoons strong coffee

stone Street, Sheffield.

Pinstone Street Sheffield, not far from Paradise Street, in 1900 shows some fine buildings and on the right Madame Rose's shop, "Ladies Modist" where the latest fashions were available. Across the road a Grand Sale is in progress offering hardware and the new, black-leaded, closed cooking range, all a far cry from country cousins who still prepared meals in a large, iron cooking pot slung over an open wood or coal fire in a room that served as kitchen, dining room, living room and bedroom for three generations of the family.

In 1900 Oxo was introduced and became a favourite ingredient in soups. Pascall's portable jellies and blancmanges and Edwards' desiccated soups were helpful additions. A Sheffield dish sold in shops was "hot udder".

61

NELLIE'S BRAMBLE JELLY

From the lanes of the Fylde of Lancashire, schoolchildren during the late summer of 1918 picked 2 cwt. of blackberries. I expect it was much the same after a good summers "blegging" in Yorkshire. Certainly there survive recipes using this luscious free fruit, nature's bounty, yet another way of eking out the family budget. Pots of bramble jelly and jam lasted well after Christmas and were useful to make a drink for sore throats or to be eaten, generous portions of the jelly with the ice cream that follows. The proportion of blackberries to sugar is:

4 lb. blackberries
4 lb. apples

Allow 1 lb. sugar to each pint of juice. The fruit should be boiled for an hour in the water and allowed to drip all night through a jelly bag. Next day add sugar to juice. Reheat, boil for 10 minutes and pot.

1 pint water

OLD-FASHIONED CUSTARD ICE CREAM

Heat ¹/₂ pint of milk with 1 oz. sugar and a vanilla pod. Stir in 2 egg yolks and 1 whole small egg beaten. Cook this custard in the top of a double saucepan, the lower part containing gently bubbling water. Stir steadily and remove from heat as soon as it thickens. Remove the vanilla pod; these are now quite expensive. Dry it and store in a jar.

Whip ¹/₂ pint cream and fold it into the custard. Pour into ice trays and freeze. When half-frozen, tip back into a basin, whip it and return to trays in refrigerator. This improves smoothness of texture. The ice cream is ready in 3 hours.

St. Leger Week – Doncaster.

Doncaster Racecourse is the home of the St. Leger Stakes
which has been run every September since 1776 and is four
years older than the well known Derby horse race at Epsom
Downs. This postcard of St. Leger Week at Doncaster dates
from September 1907. Oatcakes and gingerbread would be
on sale at the many booths near the race course to feed the
crowds coming from Sheffield 22 miles away.

BINGLEY REDCURRANT COBBLER

Place the washed redcurrants into a buttered dish, sprinkle with lemon juice and dot a little butter on the surface of the fruit. Rub the butter into the flour and add the cinnamon. Stir in the sugar, add a little water and roll out a top which fits your dish. Press on top of fruit and turn edges. Prick with a fork and bake at 200° C. This is delicious with clotted cream, double cream or ice cream.

1 lb. redcurrants
squeeze of lemon juice
4 oz. butter
6 oz. flour
pinch of cinnamon
4 oz. sugar

TODMORDEN PLUM CAKE

Line a 6 inch cake tin with greaseproof paper. Beat butter and sugar until light and creamy. Beat in the eggs one at a time then fold in sieved flour and dried fruit. Bake for 1¹/₂ hours in a slow oven 160°C.

4 oz. butter
4 oz. brown sugar
2 large eggs
6 oz. S.R. flour
6 oz. dried fruit

I remember eating this cake made simply from an old family recipe, whilst resting on a seat at the foot of Barbon Fell placed there in memory of Harry William Hardy, who died from an accident while farming on his estancia in Argentina. He was a great-grandson of Rev. Joseph Hardy, 1723-86, who was born in Barbon and whose forefathers for centuries held land there and in Mansergh by the custom of Border Tenant right.

DONCASTER PEPPER CAKE

Rub the butter into the flour and add the sugar and ground cloves. Put the baking powder in with the flour mix, treacle and eggs. Mix all well together and place mixture in a well-greased tin. Bake in a moderate oven for half an hour.

2 beaten eggs

12 oz. golden syrup or treacle

4 oz. butter

12 oz. flour

4 oz. Barbados sugar

$^1/_2$ teaspoon baking powder

$^1/_2$ oz. ground cloves

This photograph from 100 years ago of Redcar, looking along the Esplanade, is accompanied by the legend, "Visitors are unanimous in praise of the fine air, broad sands, picturesque cliffs, and ravines", when Redcar and Saltburn were reached in six hours by the Great Northern Railway from London. It dates from 1842 as a watering place famed for magnificent sands so firm that neither horse nor man could leave an imprint upon them.

BAILDON BRANDY SNAPS

Fairs all over Yorkshire sold brandy snaps at one time. Wyke Fair was especially famed for them.

Melt syrup, sugar and butter. Add the rest of the ingredients. Mix well, dropping teaspoons of this mixture onto a greased baking sheet and allowing room for each to spread. Cook for no more than 6 minutes in a moderate oven until set. Remove, cool a little, then shape into curls. My Todmorden grandmother used the scrubbed handle of a wooden spoon to shape the snaps.

2 oz. each of flour, butter sugar

2 tablespoons golden syrup

1½ teaspoons powdered ginger

1 tablespoon brandy

The old Manor House and Church Tower are photographed from Riverside, Knaresborough, in the 1930s, an ancient Royal Borough where the River Nidd has cut through limestone. In the 15th century a noted prophetess, Mother Shipton, lived in a cave by the river. At the Dropping Well articles hung under the limestone cliff eventually transform to stone by the spring waters. Nearby Harrogate was reported by James Baines as having 25 springs of curative iron and sulphur waters in the 1830s.

HARROGATE TART

Mix the flour to a smooth paste with cold milk and stir in the egg yolks. Mix in the beaten egg and sugar, stirring continually. Melt the butter in the hot milk then stir this into the egg mixture. Do this very gradually. Put this mixture into a double boiler and cook until it resembles smooth cream but do not let it boil. Remove from heat and beat in the ground almonds. The traditional Harrogate Tart was made by pouring this into a baked pastry flan case but we liked it in individual glasses with cream and ratafia biscuits.

3 egg yolks
1 pint hot milk
1 oz. butter
1 whole egg
3 oz. flour
3 oz. caster sugar
4 oz. ground almonds

ORANGE CUSTARD

The rind of half a Seville orange should be boiled until tender then beaten to a paste by a pestle and mortar. Add one spoonful of brandy, the juice of one Seville orange, 4 oz. of lump sugar and the beaten yolks of 4 eggs. For 10 minutes beat all together then pour in one pint of boiling cream. Keep on beating until the custard is cold. Put into custard cups and let them stand in a dish of boiling water until they are thick. Decorate with slices of preserved orange peel. This is a very special custard which was made over 100 years ago.

BREAD AND BUTTER PUDDING

Slice bread, spread with butter and lay in a dish with currants between each layer. Pour over this a milk custard and let it soak well into the bread. Bake in a slow oven. (1 hour)

BARLEY PUDDING

Boil 4 oz. barley until tender in milk. Drain off any superfluous milk and beat into the barley a pint of cream and two beaten eggs with 4 oz. sugar and a little nutmeg. One spoonful of rose water with 4 oz. melted butter should then be gently folded in. Cover for one hour, stirring often, then bake in a buttered dish for ¹/₂ hour in a slow oven.

4 oz. barley
1 pt. cream
2 eggs
4 oz. sugar
1 tsp. rosewater
4 oz. melted butter
milk
a little nutmeg

SKIPTON STRAWBERRY SHORTCAKE

Cream the butter and sugar. Add the beaten eggs and gradually the sieved flour, cornflour and baking powder. Place the mixture in sandwich tins lined with greaseproof paper. Smooth flat the tops and bake until golden brown in a moderate oven.

4 oz. butter
4 oz. caster sugar
2 eggs
4 oz. S.R. flour
2 oz. cornflour
1 teaspoon baking powder

Filling

Whip the cream in one bowl and the egg white in another. Fold together. Cover one shortcake with strawberries and cream. Top with the second shortcake and the rest of the cream and strawberries. Scatter the sugar upon this.

fresh strawberries
¹/₄ pint thick cream
1 egg white
a little sugar

The Denby Dale Pie of August 4th. 1928, "the largest pie in the world", helped to raise £1,000 for Huddersfield Infirmary. The Pelican Engineering Company Ltd. of Leeds were sponsors of the idea and the pie was transported by T.B. and H. Firth. Judging by the accompanying scenes, at some stage it was portioned out and eaten, perhaps cooked according to the recipe herewith for "a genuine Yorkshire pork pie", as that came from Huddersfield.

KETTLEWELL OATCAKE

Stir together all the ingredients, the yeast having been crumbled into a little tepid (not hot) milk. Mix together and shape gently. Leave covered in a warm place to allow time for the yeast to work. After half an hour cover a board with coarse oatmeal. Making an oval shape, pour on a quantity of batter. Yorkshire oatcakes ideally were cooked on a heated backstone or on the floor of the fire oven. Having shaped the oval oatcake they were flung onto the backstone but could nowadays be cooked on a griddle.

1 ¹/₂ lb. fine oatmeal
¹/₂ oz. yeast
1 pint warm water
¹/₄ teaspoon salt

One of the finest "green roads" or pack horse train roads in the Pennines curves over the moors from Kettlewell. This oatcake must have been a favourite with the drovers.

Grinton parish had its corpseway. From the lonely farmhouses the dead were carried in panniers for burial. It was a long way to church, perhaps ten miles or more. From Upper Swaledale long, slow-moving trains of jagger ponies carried lead ingots to the nearest port, from where they were shipped.

*Fishing was more than a pastime in Tudor Yorkshire, when twice-weekly
fish days occurred. On Lenten fasts and Saints' Days the eating of fish was
compulsory. Inland families had to eat smoked or salted fish unless they
could catch it fresh. March and April were lean months for food, too late
for meat slaughtered before Christmas and too soon for Spring crops. There
would be no problem of obtaining fish over the centuries at Flamborough,
photographed in 1895, whose name seems to indicate that its bold
promontory was once the site of a burning warning beacon. Discussing
food in the Yorkshire words, "looanies" were said to be eaten by labourers
and farmers leaning against stooks of corn at harvest time, but I never did
find out how they were made.*

71

COVERDALE FRUIT FLAPJACKS

Grease a shallow non-stick tin. In a large saucepan place margarine, golden syrup and caster sugar and stir over gentle heat until sugar has been dissolved. Mix together with the dry ingredients and bake in centre of oven at 180° C. for 12-15 minutes.

4¹/₂ oz. margarine

4¹/₂ oz. caster sugar

2 oz. sultanas

2 oz. cherries washed and chopped

4 oz. cornflakes

2 large tablespoons golden syrup

8 oz. porridge oats

RICH CABINET PUDDING FROM SEDBERGH

Grease a 2 pint basin with butter and line base with a circle of greaseproof paper upon which are laid a few halved cherries and angelica. Chop the remaining cherries and angelica. Break up sponge cakes and crush ratafias. Mix with the cherries and angelica and put in the basin. Lightly whisk the eggs and sugar. Heat cream to boiling point. Stir into the egg mixture and add the vanilla and brandy. Strain into the basin and leave to stand for ¹/₂ hour. Cover with buttered paper and steam the pudding for 1 hour.

This pudding may also be served with wine sauce.

4 oz. glacé cherries

1 oz. angelica

7 small sponge cakes

1 oz. ratafias

5 eggs

4 oz. caster sugar

1 pint single cream

4 drops vanilla essence

2 tablespoons brandy

Arthur Mee described Glaisdale in the 1930s as "shut off from the world by moors". Visitors came to shoot grouse or to fish rivers for trout and salmon, enjoying home-made bread, sweet oatcakes, apricot jam, apple pie and cheese in front of an open fire in the evening, feet on a "hookey" rug, but they were few and far between until powerful motor cars were invented to swoop up the "brant" slopes that had previously deterred. Our base was often Kirkby Lonsdale, where this view through the arch, looking up the Lune at Devil's Bridge, was taken by Lilywhites in the 1920s.

RUM MOUSSE

Using a pan of hot water or a double saucepan melt the chocolate in a bowl. Stir in the rum and the butter. Remove from heat. Beat the egg yolks thoroughly and gently stir into the chocolate mixture. The egg whites should be whisked until stiff and folded into the chocolate. The mousse should then be quickly poured into a wetted mould or individual glasses and left at the bottom of the fridge after decorating with the chopped nuts.

6 oz. chocolate

2 teaspoons rum

2 eggs, separated

chopped cashew nuts or walnuts

1 teaspoon unsalted butter

DATE FLAPJACK

Mix together 9 oz. dates and 4^1/2 teaspoons orange juice as filling.

Melt gently the margarine, syrup and sugar. Mix the oats, coconut and flour together with the bicarb and vanilla. Make a well in the centre of this mix and gradually add the melted ingredients. Stir well and pour into a greased, shallow tin on top of the date mixture. Cook for 35 minutes at 180°C. or gas 4.

9 oz. margarine

8 oz. caster sugar

4^1/2 oz. coconut

^{1}/2 teaspoon bicarb of soda

1^1/2 dessertspoons syrup

6 oz. rolled oats

4^1/2 oz. plain flour

1 teaspoon vanilla

9241. BRIDLINGTON: BAYLE GATE.

*Bayle Gate at Bridlington is the gatehouse of the 14th.
century Priory Church and is today the Bayle Museum,
displaying dolls' furniture, weapon and jewellery. "Cobles",
open-decked fishing boats, leave from the bustling harbour
of this seaside town where fresh fish dishes and seafood are
specialities. Bursting from the chalk hills running inland
from Flamborough Head and Bridlington are the Gypseys or
intermittent streams which flow into the sea, the most
celebrated entering the sea at Bridlington Quay.*

We were delighted to receive by post a version of burnt cream from Christopher Biggins who played Sarah the Cook in the pantomime Dick Whittington and his Cat at the Alhambra Theatre, Bradford, December 1988 - February 1989.

CREME BRULEE

Put the cream in the top half of a large double boiler or in a bowl over a pan of gently simmering water. Carefully stir the egg yolks beaten with the caster sugar and vanilla essence into the warm cream. Continue cooking gently until the cream has thickened enough to coat the back of the wooden spoon. Strain the cream through a fine sieve into a large souffle dish or mould and leave to chill for at least four hours. Then make a golden brown toffee with the Demerara sugar and pour this mixture over the top. Replace in refrigerator until required. Christopher recommended more vanilla essence but as it is so concentrated, this becomes a matter of taste. I always tend to go easy on essences and herbs.

2¹/₂ pints single cream

12 egg yolks

2 level tablespoons caster sugar

1 teaspoon vanilla essence

4 level tablespoons Demerara sugar

PARKIN

Sift flour and ginger into baking bowl then add the oatmeal. Rub in the butter and dripping, meanwhile having the treacle slowly warming. Stir in the treacle and dissolve the soda in a little warm milk. Put in all other ingredients, beating the eggs in well, and lastly adding the bicarbonate of soda in the milk. Cook slowly until firm in well-buttered square tins.

1 lb. medium oatmeal
1 lb. fine oatmeal
2 lb. treacle
3 eggs
1 oz. ground ginger
8 oz. butter
4 oz. dripping
1 lb. flour
3 teaspoons bicarbonate of soda

This old recipe involves large quantities as it was usual to make plenty. Families were big and there were sometimes farm workers to feed as well.

George Bousfield from the Market Square, Kirkby Stephen, invited us into his home, dated 1636, which had once been the Old Fountain Inn. George lives opposite a square once famous for bear-baiting. His family had farmed land and kept an inn well known for its home brewed ale and parkin. The signs above the dated door lintel, a star and a flower, which had puzzled George for some time, were probably to keep away witches, the custom of 350 years ago.

The York - London Royal Mail Coach in the Dales of the late 18th. century. Beautifully matched, mettlesome teams of horses were used in the large towns, but the last day of the month, known as magazine night, was the hardest time of all for the horses as coaches were in addition laden with periodicals. Some died in harness from overwork; others were sold for as little as one guinea when they could no longer cope with the journeys at speed. Weary passengers were often as hungry as wolves when they arrived at the coaching inns, the best of which served far-famed food such as York Hams. Coaching inns were open 24 hours a day but stops for passengers were short as a strict schedule had to be observed.

LEYBURN SHERRY BISCUITS

Rub butter into flour until it looks like breadcrumbs. Stir in caster sugar and grated rind of ¹/₂ lemon. Mix to a dough with 2 egg yolks and sherry. Dust the pastry board with rice flour and roll out ¹/₄ inch thick. Cut into 3 inch rounds with a pastry cutter. Bake in a moderate oven for 10 minutes. Mix the icing sugar with the squeezed lemon juice. Coat the biscuits with this warmed icing, sprinkling each with a scatter of the other half of grated lemon rind.

4 oz. butter
¹/₂ lb. plain flour
2 eggs
1 lemon
3 oz. caster sugar
1 tablespoon sherry
4 oz. icing sugar

JAM BISCUITS

Mix together to form a dough, roll out, cut thinly into circles and bake in a moderate oven for about 10 minutes. Sandwich them together in pairs with strawberry jam when cool.

8 oz. S.R. flour
4 oz. sugar
4 oz. butter
1 egg
¹/₄ teaspoon baking powder

"I have been trying to remember the things my mother cooked but many are now not available, for all those lovely dishes were cooked on an open fire range. Tripe and Onions, Oxtail Soup, Giblet Pie, Rabbit and Fowl Pie, Baked Stuffed Marrow, Leek and Shallot Pasties. For a treat on Sundays we had a boiled Roly Poly Pudding ..."

A cheerful group of woollen mill workers at Mirfield early this century, although there was not much to be cheerful about as the mill was due to close. The part each operative played in manufacture is indicated by what they held: spindles, cops, unspun wool, packing. The man at the back must be the "gaffer", strict to the minute over meal breaks and arrival time.

ROLY POLY PUDDING

Mix these ingredients together with a little milk to make a soft dough. Add the milk carefully, a little at a time. Roll out and spread with a favourite jam (blackberry was ours) and roll up like a Swiss Roll. Roll into a floured cloth and tie up the ends with string. Boil for $^1/_2$ hour. We ate it with cream.

8 oz. flour

4 oz. suet

2 oz. brown sugar

2 teaspoons baking powder

DAMASK JUNKET

Bring the single cream to blood heat, adding sugar. Stir in the rennet. Pour into the serving dish and allow it to clot, sprinkling the nutmeg all over the surface. Before serving, mix together the 4 tablespoons of double cream, the rose water and 1 tablespoon caster sugar and pour over the junket.

2 heaped tablespoons caster sugar

$^1/_4$ teaspoon ground nutmeg

1 teaspoon rennet

1 pint single cream

3 teaspoons rose water

4 tablespoons double cream

This recipe dates back to the 18th. century when cream and roses were plentiful. Aunt Kate used rose petals from full-blown flowers to set off the delicate texture of this sweet.

Junkets are quick to make, light and easy to digest. As a variant, 1 tablespoon of brandy could be added and the rose water omitted.

*The harbour at Bridlington Quay, shown in 1902, could
hold 200 vessels, the only harbour between Leith and
Harwich it was possible to enter during northerly gales, as
the Bay gave shelter till the tide allowed entrance. The two
stone piers have examples of both sail and steam. From this
harbour a good view of Flamborough Head was obtainable.*

Drinks, etc

LEMONADE
TO BE MADE THE DAY BEFORE

Pare 24 lemons thinly, putting the peel from 8 into 3 quarts of hot, not boiling water. Cover for 4 hours. Rub fine sugar onto the lemons and squeeze their juice into a china bowl. Add 1^1/$_2$ lbs. of fine sugar and the water in which the lemon rinds have been steeping. Next pour on 1 pint of boiling water, mix, strain and leave for 24 hours - another good old remedy for sore throats or feverish childish ailments.

GINGER BEER

In 3 quarts of the water boil the bruised ginger for ^{1}/$_2$ hour, then add sugar, lemon juice and honey plus the rest of the water. Strain. When cold, add a quarter of the white of an egg and a small teaspoon of essence of lemon. Allow all to stand for 4 days and bottle. This keeps for months.

2^1/$_2$ lb. sugar
2 dessertspoons lemon juice
2 oz. honey
2^1/$_2$ oz. bruised ginger root
4^1/$_2$ gallons water

TREACLE BEER

Put the treacle into the boiling water and stir until well mixed, then add the cold water and the yeast. Place in a large, earthenware basin and cover with a cloth doubled twice. The next day it can be bottled.

1 lb. treacle
2 quarts boiling water
8 quarts cold water
1 teacup yeast

I have never made this beer, which dates from the 19th. century. The amount of yeast "can be substituted with a pint of brisk stout". It sounds like old Cornish beer which was called Mahogany and also made with treacle.

*A 1904 postcard of Huddersfield shows the imposing London
and Midland Bank, Dawson's shirt makers and a large shop
sign, "Manfield's Special Boot Sale Today". Wool has been
spun and woven around Huddersfield for centuries, a
cottage craft from the moorlands until the 18th. century.
The Cloth Hall was built as centre for the Industry in 1776
but pulled down in 1930. The 19th. century Town Hall,
another imposing Yorkshire building, is the home of the
famous Huddersfield Choral Society.*

HOME BREWED ALE

"Take 2 gallons of hot water and add 2 pecks of malt. Stir well then add 8 gallons more hot water. Cover with a cloth and stand for 3 hours, then sieve to remove grains. Place the liquor in a boiler and when it boils add 4 oz. hops. Continue to boil for 1 hour then run off into a fermenting barrel. Cover with a cloth and allow to cool until it is barely warm. It is now ready for ¹/₂ pint fresh brewer's yeast. Stir well, cover vessel with a cloth and allow to ferment for 12-15 hours. Strain the home-brewed beer through a hair sieve to remove yeast and fill the barrel. It can be drunk after a week but improves with keeping."

Instructions from 1900.

CLEAT WINE

This is one of the old recipes for wines made by Granny Robson who lived at Robin Hood's Bay. The one for Cleat Wine was delicious, but cleats don't grow in abundance in meadows as they used to.

4 pint pots of flower heads
4 quarts water
3 lemons
1 oz. ginger
3¹/₂ lb. sugar
¹/₂ oz. yeast

Put flowers in bowl. Pour over the boiling water. Leave three days. Stir every day. Strain then boil liquid with lemon juice and rind. Add sugar and ginger. Add yeast last when just warm. Leave two days. Bottle and leave to ferment. Do not make corks tight for a week or two.

ITALIAN GARDENS, SOUTH CLIFF, SCARBOROUGH.

Of Scarborough by the 18th. century it was claimed that "most of the gentry of the north of England and Scotland resort here". There was horse-racing on the sands, theatre, dancing, gaming rooms and a circulating library, "one of the most ancient and respectable sea-bathing places in Great Britain", where 26 bathing machines lined up. Already a spa town, Scarborough was unique as being able to offer both spa and sea water. In this picture postcard a fashionable group chat together in the Italian Gardens in 1925.

87

BEETROOT TONIC
(FOR ANAEMIC TEENAGERS) 1920

Wash a pound of beetroot and cut into slices.
Put in earthenware bowl. Cover with a pound
of Demerara sugar. Leave to stand for 24-36
hours, then strain the liquid and add a pint
bottle of stout. A wine glass each day.

PORT WINE
(ELDER FLOWERS)

Boil together ¹/₂ hour. When cold, strain and
bottle.

1 quart elder juice

4 lb. sugar

1 gallon cold water

¹/₄ oz. powder alum

1 good handful logwood chips

RASPBERRY WINE

4 pints juice from raspberries - strain through
muslin, allow to drip. Add 1¹/₂ lb. sugar. Stir until
dissolved. Cover and allow to stand for 4 days.
Stir twice daily. Strain and add one wine glass
of brandy. Bottle and cork tightly. Keep for three
months.

HERB BEER

Boil washed nettles and dandelion flowers in water for ¹/₂ hour. Strain off and add sugar, ginger and yeast. Leave for 6 hours. Strain and bottle.

Skin Lotion can be made from a mixture of half and half rose water and witch hazel. It is mildly astringent. Keep in fridge.

2 lb. nettles

1¹/₂ lb. dandelion flowers

2 quarts water

¹/₂ lb. sugar

1 teaspoon ground ginger

1 oz. yeast

FENNEL WATER

"A tonic and antiseptic lotion for the skin: Sling a handful of fennel in a pint and half of water and bring to the boil. Simmer for 15 minutes then cool and store in a clean bottle. This must be used in 10 days unless kept in fridge."

A photograph taken almost a century ago. On the right is Granny Robson whose recipe for Cleat Wine is included in this book. This great Yorkshire cook also made Brawn from a recipe passed down from her mother, who may be the lady seated, knitting, on the left. This old cottage at Robin Hood's Bay has since, through cliff erosion, fallen into the sea.

NETTLE BEER

A great favourite in early Spring for "clearing the blood".

Into 2 gallons of water place and boil several handfuls of fresh, young, stinging nettles, a few handfuls of dandelion leaves, a few handfuls of cleavers (called goosegrass in some areas) and 2 oz. of bruised ginger. Boil all together for half an hour and strain. On pieces of toasted bread spread some brewer's yeast, then float these on the beer to commence working. When the fermentation is over, i.e. when no more bubbles are rising, add 1 oz. cream of tartar. Bottle and cork the beer, laying bottles on side in a rack. The nettle beer can be drunk in a few days.

Recipes for "primmie rose wine" (primrose) would not be allowed these days. The nature wardens would be on our tracks, but we can still pick a few nettles away from the car fumes.

Now a Youth Centre, Marrick Priory in its lonely setting of the middle reaches of Swaledale, since the 12th. century provided corn, fish from one of the swiftest rivers in England, fleeces from large flocks and cheese made from ewes' milk. The nuns' home-brewed ale and nettle beer was part of their hospitality for travellers.

OVEN TEMPERATURE CHART

C.	F.	Gas No.	Description
110	225	$1/4$	Very slow
120/130	250	$1/2$	Very slow
140	275	1	Slow
150	300	2	Slow
160/170	325	3	Moderate
180	350	4	Moderate
190	375	5	Moderately hot
200	400	6	Moderately hot
220	425	7	Hot
230	450	8	Hot
240	475	9	Very hot

TABLE OF EQUIVALENT MEASURES AND WEIGHTS

1 Breakfast of fluids equals, approximately		¹/₂ pints
1 Teacupful	:	¹/₄ pints
3 Tablespoonfuls	:¹/₂ teacupful or	¹/₈ pint
1 Teacupful flour or chopped suet	:	¹/₄ lb.
1 Small teacupful sugar	:	¹/₄ lb.
1 Teacupful butter	:	¹/₄ lb.
1 Teacupful breadcrumbs	:	2 oz.
1 Tablespoonful Golden Syrup	:	2 oz.
1 Heaped Tablespoonful flour or chopped suet	:	1 oz.
1 Level tablespoonful sugar	:	1 oz.
1 Level tablespoonful butter	:	1 oz.
1 Dessertspoonful	:	¹/₂ tablespoonful

acknowledgements

High on the list are grateful thanks to an indispensable chauffeur and food taster, my willing husband, cheerful companion and adviser in all jaunts. Together we share happy memories of Yorkshire friendliness and kindness as legendary as the cooking. I particularly thank the following past and present friends and relations who have made this book possible:

Sarah Anderson; Nellie Bates; Helen Betts; Christopher Biggins; George Bousfield; Glyn Burgess; Stan Butterworth; the late Richard Clegg; Jean and Gordon Dearden; the late Cecil F. Doughty; Bill Duerden; the late Emma Fielden; Bob Gibson; Norah Green; Ronald Harker; Esther Hendy; Phyllis Hicks; the late Ethel Houghton; Joan Ibbetson; Des Layton; Del Lister; Louise Mc Kie; the late Fred Mills; North Yorkshire County Library; Alice Nightingale; John and Mary Parkin; Mr. C.J. Plummer; John Richards; Ron Severs; West Yorkshire Library Service; Diana Wright; Bill Yates; "May" from Shipley.